The Joy of Easter

Devotions for Lent

Peter Caligiuri

The Joy of Easter by Peter Caligiuri © 2021
Edited by Nancy Caligiuri
ISBN: 9798401256119
All Creatures Mostly Small publishing
Showing our Big God in the Smallest Details of Life

Scripture quotations from KJV and The Holy Bible, English Standard Version. ESV® Text Edition: 2016. Copyright © 2001 by Crossway Bibles, a publishing ministry of Good News Publishers.

All rights reserved no parts of this publication may be reproduced, stored in a retrieval system or transmitted in any form or by any means except for brief quotations in printed reviews without the prior permission of the author.

This Book Belongs To

Presented by

Introduction - What Exactly is Lent?

They that wait upon the Lord shall renew their strength. They shall mount up with wings like eagles. They shall run and not be weary. They shall walk and not faint. **Isaiah 40:31 KJV**

So, you might ask, "What exactly is Lent?" That is one great question with more than one answer! In general, Lent is the time from Ash Wednesday until either the Wednesday before Easter, Holy Saturday or Easter Sunday depending on which tradition you follow. You also might wonder why we should observe this 40-day period since there is no record of anyone in the Bible doing so. For starters, it is never a bad idea to set aside special times for seeking God's will and purpose. Some call it, "Waiting on the Lord." Waiting in the right way, comes with God's promise of strength and renewal. Some of you may choose to fast certain foods or to do special acts of service, during these weeks. However, you choose to honor the season, the most important thing of all is to focus on Jesus. For me personally Easter brings back the excitement of my coming to faith in Jesus on Easter Sunday! So during Lent, I come to each morning with an open heart, asking Jesus for a brand new insight into His word and for His will for that day. My suggestion is that instead of racing ahead or lagging behind in your devotional readings, why not slow down and listen to what God is saying? Walking with Jesus will lead you along the path that He has chosen, and following that path will bring you to the destination He has for your life. My prayer is that together during Lent, we may again see the miracles of Jesus, the table of His Last Supper, the Cross, the empty grave and most of all, our Risen Lord!

Day 1　Ash Wednesday
The Marks of Jesus

From henceforth let no man trouble me: for I bear in my body the marks of the Lord Jesus. **Galatians 6:17 KJV**

Though Paul carried the marks of the beatings that he received for the cause of Christ - not the sign of the cross in ashes on his head - nevertheless, there is nothing forbidden about receiving ashes as a way of identifying with Jesus during Lent. After all, the very word," Christian" means a follower of Christ. During these next six and a half weeks, we are choosing to remind ourselves that following Jesus is the most important thing in life.

Either wearing a cross or receiving the mark of the cross in ashes, is our way of remembering that Jesus came to die so that we could live. First, why not ask ourselves during Lent, "What kind of life does He want me to lead? Secondly,

Lent can be the time when we renew the most important relationship of all, "Our relationship with God." Everything that Jesus did, everything He suffered, everything was so that our relationship could be restored. So, if this relationship was more important to Jesus than His own life, then let's open our hearts wide on this journey towards the cross, the tomb and resurrection morning!

Day 2
Amazing – Extraordinary Love!

For as high as the heavens are above the earth, so great is his steadfast love toward those who fear him - But the steadfast love of the Lord is from everlasting to everlasting on those who fear him, and his righteousness to children's children.
Psalm 103:11; 17 ESV

The difference between God's love and ours is that His stretches far beyond our horizon, while ours falls flat on its face on the way out the door. Our love can be here today and gone tomorrow but His love is eternal and extends to our children, grandchildren, neighbors and even our enemies. God's love is more than just a passionate emotion; it is a dynamic power. God's love stirs everything and everyone it touches into action. God's love forms planets and feeds the hungry. The love of Jesus transforms water into wine and murderers, like the Apostle Paul into messengers of Christ and martyrs for the faith. During Lent, we often consider what things to give up. Maybe we should instead think about what we will give. Let's ask ourselves, "What new challenge will God give me this year and how can I show the amazing, extraordinary love to others, that He showed us all at the cross?"

Day 3   For the Joy

Looking unto Jesus the author and finisher of our faith; who for the joy that was set before him endured the cross, despising the shame, and is set down at the right hand of the throne of God.
Hebrews 11:2 KJV

Today's verse tells us that the joy set before Jesus gave Him strength to endure the cross. For most of us, joy means big events like winning the super bowl, walking down the aisle at our wedding or seeing the birth of our child. But in the darkness and cold, with His body weakened from blood loss and shock from the beatings, a different kind of joy helped Jesus endure. Maybe that joy was a kind that included a long list of little events that gave Him strength. Little events; like being mistaken for the gardener working away, until only Mary Magdalene remained at the tomb and then hearing the astonishment and joy in her voice as He called her by name. Small joys sustained Him, like hiding His smile while He walked with His disciples to Emmaus listening to them argue over the wild reports the women gave about meeting angels at His tomb. Maybe Jesus imagined the sudden change of expression on Thomas' face when he saw the marks of the nails, or the sight of Peter leaping from the boat when he realized that it was Jesus who had filled his net with fish. This joy was the joy of millions of little moments in all of us who have believed and it carried Jesus through the suffering and shame of Calvary. One by one throughout the ages, when we see Him and believe, that joy lives again both in His heart and in ours. What a Savior! What a joy! What amazing love!

What if Joy?

When pain pulls down the window shade
Through which our hope might see
What if joy's the path God give for us
To follow and be free?

There God in grace bends down to lift
Our earthbound looking eyes
So we can see the mountain peaks
Over which His wings can fly!

So, no hiding in a corner or
Sailing far across the seas
Don't miss the path of joy on which
Our faith in laughter leads!

For God in grace bends down to lift
Our earthward looking eyes
So we can see the mountain peaks
Over which His wings can fly!

Day 4   Made For Life

Then the angel showed me the river of the water of life, bright as crystal, flowing from the throne of God and of the Lamb through the middle of the street of the city. **Revelation 22:1 ESV**

It seems strange, though at my age it should not be, to realize that so many of my family and my friends have gone into eternity. That sobering thought turns me to wondering what it will be like in my own last moments here and first moments with God. How brave will I be when I put my foot into the boat that will take me across God's great river? For the Christian there is no fear in death, yet it still seems so wrong – so unnatural – so contrary to the joy of life that is seated deep within our hearts no matter our age. Then one day it came to me; that, death feels unnatural because God made us for life!

Everything in heaven is about life. Jesus is the way the truth and the LIFE. The words He spoke were Spirit and LIFE. He offers a drink of LIVING water and whoever believes in Him will not perish but have eternal LIFE. There is nothing in God's plan that has anything whatsoever to do with death. We must choose to live every day with our focus on life, because that is what He created us for. We may no longer be strong, but the strength of the life of Christ is greater in weakness. We might not be able to do certain things easily, but we can do all things through Christ. Then one day, in the words of the Apostle Paul, when death has been swallowed up in victory we will be changed from this life to the next. Depression and the fear of death lose their grip when we remember that Jesus has a life to give us that is more abundant and overflowing that we could ever imagine!

Day 5   Three Short Days

Now on the first day of the week Mary Magdalene came to the tomb early, while it was still dark, and saw that the stone had been taken away from the tomb **John 20:1 ESV**

Sometimes in Winter when I hear of snow falling everywhere except Florida, I remember that the year before we moved here, our hometown of Scranton was buried under twenty-four inches of snow. Cars were completely covered; our street was closed for two days and everyone's schedule came to a screeching halt! But then just three weeks later, with the temperatures reaching 80 degrees, the snow vanished. What a difference those three short weeks made!

One Friday night two thousand years ago, the disciples hid in fear. Then Joseph and Nicodemus took Jesus down from the cross and put Him into the tomb. For everyone who loved Him it seemed that all their hopes lay cold and dead in His grave. But very early in the morning of the third day, when Mary came, she discovered in astonishment that the stone had been rolled back and the grave stood empty! When Jesus Himself drew near, Mary mistook Him for the gardener. Just like us she had only seen Him as a great teacher a wonderful man or an amazing healer, but when she saw Him alive, for the first time she knew Him as the Son of God. Now after two thousand years we are all still amazed at all that changed in just three short days!

Day 6 The Road That Lies Ahead

And it came to pass, that, while they communed together and reasoned, Jesus himself drew near, and went with them. **Luke 24:15 KJV**

Sometimes we look at Easter as a single defining event of our faith. But the Good News of Easter morning is that, as we walk (or run in Peter's case) from the tomb, Jesus comes and walks with us. If we believe that living for Jesus means we have to do everything just right, then we will often want to give up. You should be encouraged to know that on the first Easter, Jesus decided to walk with disciples who were far from perfect. Let's listen in on their conversation a bit:

But we had hoped that he was the one to redeem Israel…. **Luke 24:21 ESV**

In other words; they had given up hope. They just didn't get it. Why had Jesus died? On those kinds of days Jesus draws near and asks:

Was it not necessary that the Christ should suffer these things and enter into his glory? **Luke 24:26 ESV**

Just like a doctor treating a wound Jesus pokes and prods with questions that can make us feel uncomfortable. But His examination is for the purpose of healing and focusing our thinking on Hs cross, His forgiveness and eternal life.

Prayer: Father my hope this morning is no longer that I have everything right, but that You will come along side today. Come Lord and walk alongside me to the cross that meant death for You and eternal life for me.

Day 7
Complaint Department Upstairs

Then Jesus calling out with a loud voice said, "Father into Your hands I commit my spirit!" and having said this, He breathed His last. **Luke 23:46 ESV**

I have a small confession to make - there are some days that I love to complain! I complain about the weather, my church, my kids and even my wife. Some nights as I lay my head on the pillow and replay the remarks which I made, I wonder how I could have been so unkind and wish I had kept my lips sealed. Jesus on the other hand had no shortage of things to complain about. Think about it; on the worst day of his life, Jesus encouraged a thief; made sure His mother was taken care, forgave His enemies, and with his last breath trusted his life into the Father's hands. How did He do that? What was His secret?

Some years ago, I was bringing a truckload of branches to our local landfill. As I pulled up to the entrance of the one-story weigh-in station I noticed a small sign by the side of the operator's window that had an arrow pointed up stating, "Complaint department upstairs!"

But how can we be patient like Jesus when others mistreat or abuse us physically or verbally? The answer is in knowing where the complaint department is located. Telling our neighbors, our family, or our enemies the way we feel does not help. Remember those WWJD bracelets we used to wear in Sunday school? They asked the question; "What would Jesus do?" Well today's verse reminds us of what Jesus did - He gave His life trusting God would work all things together for good. So maybe, just maybe, if we stopped looking for the complaint department and started trusting everything into God's hands, we might be amazed at what He could do today!

Day 8   Something More

Just as day was breaking, Jesus stood on the shore; yet the disciples did not know that it was Jesus. When they got out on land, they saw a charcoal fire in place, with fish laid out on it, and bread **John 21:4; 9 ESV**

He said to him the third time, "Simon, son of John, do you love me?" Peter was grieved because he said to him the third time, "Do you love me?" and he said to him, "Lord, you know everything; you know that I love you." Jesus said to him, "Feed my sheep. **John 21:17 ESV**

Just as He did for His disciples long ago, this morning Jesus is standing at the shores of our lives. He has watched us all night as we worked hard trying to fish without Him. He is waiting at dawn, for us to see Him and come running.

But while Jesus waited all night He wasn't resting. No! He has been busy baking fresh bread and cooking the fish He had caught. Jesus was waiting with something prepared for Peter and the disciples. Now, just as then He has blessings in store but He also has one simple question:; "Do you love Me?" If we can honestly answer as Peter, "Lord you know all things. You know that I love you."? Then, He asks us something more: "Feed my sheep!" and "Follow Me!"

Day 9
Jesus Loves Mundane Details!

They said to him, "Where will you have us prepare it?" He said to them "Behold, when you have entered the city, a man carrying a jar of water will meet you. Follow him into the house that he enters. **Luke 22:9-10 ESV**

In our extended family which includes two grown sons, two daughters in law and seven grandchildren, the location of our family Thanksgiving dinner can be a subject of delicate negotiation. Lots of preparation goes into planning where to hold it, who to invite and even how the table is to be set up. I confess that instead of just a season of Thankfulness and contentment sometimes it is a struggle to just get along with people. Many of my frustrations come from struggling with mundane details that I feel God could not care about. In some ways the Passover meal was the Jewish Thanksgiving meal of the first century. So, how did the disciples get ready for it? After three and a half years of seeing bread multiplied, water changed to wine and storms calmed by a word they wisely decided to just ask Jesus what He wanted to do about the details.

No matter what you and I face today, we could take a tip from these disciples and ask Jesus to become our event planner. The same God who formed the universe also counts every hair on our heads. It is not a problem to ask Him to take control of even the mundane details of our lives. When we do, we might be amazed at how delighted He will be to show us exactly what He has planned. Every detail of our hearts matters to Him!

Day 10   Washing Feet

If I then, your Lord and Teacher, have washed your feet, you also ought to wash one another's feet.
John 13:14 ESV

One of the most overlooked events leading up to Easter is when Jesus washed His disciples' feet. A few times in my life I have been blessed to be a part of a foot washing ceremony. It has been an amazing experience, but Jesus was not talking just about a ceremony. Foot washing was simply a practical everyday need in the ancient world. People walked everywhere and the dusty streets got everyone's feet coated with dirt and grime. Washing someone else's feet would be like us going over to a friend's house to do their laundry or take out the garbage.

For most of us the challenge of foot washing is not just the job, but that of taking the position of a lowly servant. Because we associate who we are with what we do, it is easy to think that we will lose value if we begin to act like servants. But Jesus left us more than a command. He left us His example. The question then is "What is the job God has called me to do?" If He washed feet to show His love, how can I do otherwise? We can wash feet, take out the garbage or change diapers all because we love Him. We can do the small things without getting big heads and show the world, foot by foot and generation by generation the depth and the beauty of the love of God for us!

Day 11   The Service Entrance

A new commandment I give to you, that you love one another: just as I have loved you, you also are to love one another. **John 13:34 ESV**

Some years ago, I worked trimming trees on a large estate in Katonah, New York. Since the work we did was usually performed in the winter, it was a special blessing to us that tucked under one of the wings of the house was a greenhouse with a small semi-heated area where we could warm ourselves at lunch. Though we rarely saw the owner or even the caretaker we were able to get in because the spare key was kept under the edge of the fountain and it opened a door marked, "Service entrance."

Jesus gave us His command to love one another in the same way that He had loved us. If we ask, "How did Jesus love us?" we need look no further than the cross. The cross was the key to the door by which Jesus entered heaven on our behalf. If we want to follow then we need only look for where He left us the key. It is right there by the service entrance. Washing feet puts the key in the lock and opens the door for us to love God's children from every corner of the earth!

Day 12   The Captain's Voice

He said, "Come." So Peter got out of the boat and walked on the water and came to Jesus. But when he saw the wind, he was afraid, and beginning to sink he cried out, "Lord, save me." And immediately Jesus stretched out His hand and caught him, and said to him, "O you of little faith, why did you doubt?" **Matthew 14:29-31 ESV**

My grandfather, a retired Navy Captain we affectionately called Cap-Cap. We grandchildren were always amazed how, His low gravelly voice, which usually encouraged us, could in an instant change when trouble started. It was not that Cap-Cap ever shouted; rather he simply lowered his tone. Our gentle grandfather suddenly took command of the situation. "Now hear this." he would say with a ring of authority that got our attention. "Front and center!" he'd call out next and we would stop whatever mischief we were up to and come running. My grandfather's voice reminds me of Jesus calling for Peter to come to Him out on the water. Jesus didn't need to shout, because He spoke with authority. Even over the wind and waves Peter could hear that low powerful tone of His Captain's voice and it gave him the courage to obey. All of us have different conflicts that threaten to drown us under the wind and waves of circumstances. Like Peter, we are frightened, and unsure of how to walk through what lies ahead. But Jesus calls us with a voice that echoes out over our dark waters.

Its sound carries with it His authority as Captain of our lives and He calls us to come. It tells us that He is in control of our situation and waiting for us to join Him. He calls us with His promise and an assurance, that even if we should start to sink, He will be ready to pull us out and walk with us all the way to the boat!.

Day 13   Memories at the Table

And he took bread, and when he had given thanks, he broke it and gave it to them, saying, "This is my body, which is given for you. Do this in remembrance of me." **Luke 22:19**

When my mom passed away she left a few odds and ends of furniture from my great-grandmother. Besides a small side board which sat in our office for years were a few worn out chairs and some curious table leaves with legs that took up permanent residence in our attic. One night as I was reorganizing things, I began to examine the spare table parts thinking maybe I could salvage them for shelves. They seemed strangely familiar and so I paused to look more closely. Then in a flash I realized that they fit into the side board and made up the table at which I had once sat down to breakfast with my great grandmother over 60 years ago.
In that same way Jesus has left behind a table for us to remember. While my

table was a happy memory of my childhood, His was in remembrance of His cross. As journey towards His resurrection don't forget that we must first stop at the Lord's table. Let's be careful to remember Him and look forward to celebrating on Easter and the unveiling of the gift of eternal life for all who love Him and put their trust in Him!

Day 14   When He Sang

And when they had sung a hymn, they went out to the Mount of Olives.
Matthew 26:30 ESV

I am intrigued that the Bible tells us that Jesus sang. I wonder if he was a baritone or a tenor. Did he have a strong voice or were His notes a little wobbly? Jesus singing reminds me of the pastor of our church many years who sometimes got so excited about a particular praise chorus, that he would exclaim, "Let's sing it one more time for Jesus!" Some Sundays he would even call out a second time, "Let's sing it one more time for me!"

On the night that Jesus sat with His disciples at the Last Supper He also washed their feet. That same night Judas headed out the door, on his way to the Sanhedrin to betray. Jesus, knowing all this still, decided it was time to sing.

You might think that singing was a strange thing for them to do, but Jesus knew that it was the perfect time to worship. If we listen closely, we might still be able to hear His voice echoing down through time saying, "Hey guys let's sing that chorus one more time for me!"

Prayer: Father - there are some days that I feel like I am sinking into a dark pit. I know you have promised heaven, but the stuff I am facing right now on earth feels overwhelming. Help me to learn the words to the song you have for me and come sing it with me today!

Day 15   Spring Is Almost Here!

The flowers appear on the earth, the singing of birds is come, and the voice of the turtle (dove) is heard in our land. **Song of Solomon 2:12**

While our year begins in winter, with the month of January, you might be surprised to learn that the Bible's calendar begins in the spring with a month called Abib. That month was when the Jewish people celebrated the Passover, their deliverance from Egypt and their beginning as a nation. But would you be surprised to know that Abib was also the month when Jesus died? Then, in the same way that the Israelites passed through the Red Sea to their freedom, so the death of Jesus on the cross, means freedom from the power of sin over us as believers and the beginning of a new life. So, with Easter just one month away, let's pause and remember that our celebration of the resurrection of Jesus from the dead also means the celebration of the beginning of a new life. In the same way that we put a new calendar on the wall every year, why not put a fresh calendar of God's promises on the wall of your heart this year? You might just be amazed to watch as He parts the Red Sea and leads you into the freedom of a wonderful new life in Jesus Christ!

Day 16   Saint Patrick and Lent

For me to live is Christ and to die is gain. **Philippians 1:21 KJV**

It is interesting that Saint Patrick's Day often falls right in the middle of Lent. I love it because Patrick's life is a wonderful example that shows us we need both the joy of salvation and the courage of faith to fully live for Christ. It is well known that Saint Patrick brought Christianity to Ireland, but did you know that Saint Patrick, the patron saint of Ireland was actually from either England or Scotland? In fact, young Patrick's first trip to Ireland happened when he was kidnapped by a raiding party and sold as a house slave in Ireland. Patrick soon escaped his masters and was directed by a dream to a ship that just happened to be ready to sail for England. Eventually Patrick made it safely back home, but strangely enough, he soon found, God stirring his heart about the needs of the Irish people. Though Patrick struggled over the decision for months, he finally decided that it would be better to die doing what God had called him to do, than to live a safe and empty life. Saint Patrick went on to bravely bring the message of Jesus to Ireland, even converting its pagan king to Christianity. Yes, he lived an amazing life, but God has a special purpose for every one of our lives as well, and in this season of Lent what better thing could we do than to live fully just as Patrick did for the love of Jesus Christ?

I arise today through God's strength to pilot me; God's might to uphold me, God's wisdom to guide me, God's ear to hear me, God's word to speak for me, God's hand to guard me, God's way to lie before me. **Saint Patrick**

Day 17   The Donkey Waited

Now when they drew near to Jerusalem and came to Bethphage, to the Mount of Olives, then Jesus sent two disciples, saying to them, "Go into the village in front of you, and immediately you will find a donkey tied, and a colt with her. Untie them and bring them to me. **Matthew 21:1-2 ESV**

Some days I feel a lot like the donkey in this story. He had to wait for hours, tied to a post, waiting for the disciples to come. But God keeps a perfect schedule and the donkey Jesus chose has some lessons for us today.

First, he waited quietly. Imagine what might have happened if when the disciples came they heard the donkey braying loudly and wildly tugging at his reins. In the same way as the disciples were looking for a gentle animal to carry their master, so God is looking for hearts quietly waiting for His call.

Second, the donkey had to be willing to go. If the donkey started bucking and pulling in the opposite direction after they untied it, they could have brought him to Jesus. As we used to sing, "This is the day that the Lord has made." So let's gladly go in whatever direction He leads. Last of all, we can wait patiently because just like the donkey, Jesus knows exactly where we are. He hasn't forgotten us. Instead, we have been reserved for the master's use. We must wait patiently, ready to go where He calls because He remembers us and has the perfect job prepared for us to do today!

Day 18 Poured Out

I am poured out like water and all my bones are out of joint. My heart is like wax it is melted in the midst of my bowels. **Psalm 22:14 KJV**

As a teenager I always loved the Christmas presents I got from my stepmother Amy. She bought me beautiful expensive clothes, but she always left the price tag on! It was not that she minded spending the money, but she wanted to be sure that I treated her gifts with special care! In some ways God is a lot like Amy. God loves lavishing us with His grace, but He wants us to know the cost.

In the Garden of Gethsemane, Jesus said that His soul was sorrowful unto death. He agonized in prayer in order to accept the suffering of the cross. He asked if there was any other way and then sweat ran down His face like great drops of blood. Just hours after He had finished praying, Jesus was nailed to the cross. Today's Bible verse tells us that He was poured out like water. The spear pierced His side and then the last drop of the lifeblood of Jesus flowed down to the ground. What a price He paid for us! Let's be grateful to God for His blessings and treasure more greatly the gift we are given, by remembering the price that He paid.

Day 19 God's Short List

And Jesus said, "Father, forgive them, for they know not what they do." And they cast lots to divide his garments. **Luke 23:34 KJV**

Whenever the president goes about nominating anyone for service in the government, he makes up what is called a "short list" of names. These are the most qualified, smartest, and powerful folks available. In addition to their abilities they need to have no embarrassing secret past, no criminal record, or financial entanglements. Then, only after the best of the best have been looked over carefully, is the final choice made.

Luckily for us, God works in a different manner. In the New Testament, His short list of candidates included corrupt tax collectors like Zacchaeus; condemned criminals like the thief crucified next to him and even a disciple named Peter who had denied him three times. Our greatest hope at Easter, is not that God has us on His short list, but that our sins will be forgiven. We are as far from God as the soldiers who nailed His hands to the cross and Jesus reaches out to all of us in His prayer.

Do you feel far from God's plans for your life and hopelessly entangled in a lifestyle that is leading you away from Him? The best news in the universe is that Jesus has chosen to love us all, even the ones who made the crown of thorns for His head. In fact He is not just picking you to do a job for Him, He wants you as His child!

Day 20   They Put Him in the Tomb

He went to Pilate and asked for the body of Jesus. Then Pilate ordered it to be given to him. **Matthew 27:58 ESV**

The difficulty for those who claim that the resurrection is just a myth is the myriad of inconvenient eye-witness accounts. The gospel writers include all kinds of the nitty-gritty details that would only be needed in a coroner's report, not a fairy tale.

The Bible doesn't just antiseptically record that Jesus was crucified and died. We are told about the thorns on His head, the gambling for His clothing and the spear thrust into His side. When the brutal and corrupt Pontius Pilate released the body of Jesus, he ordered his soldiers to deliver it to Joseph. In other words, he wanted to be certain that He was dead.

After Jesus cried out, "Into your hands I commit my spirit" His spirit went directly into the presence of the Father, but the physical heart that had begun beating in Bethlehem was indeed completely still. There was no more breath. There were to be no more words, no tears, or laughter. The Jesus who had walked with His disciples could no longer take even one more step. He was taken down by the Romans and wrapped in linen by Joseph and Nicodemus. They gently carried His lifeless body to the tomb. They rolled the stone over the door and the soldiers sealed it and stood guard. And as far as anyone knew…that was that! Or was it?

Day 21   One Simple Miracle

But the angel said to the women, "Do not be afraid, for I know that you seek Jesus who was crucified. He is not here, for he has risen, as he said. Come, see the place where he lay. **Matthew 28:5-6 ESV**

As we get closer to Easter, we need to remember what our faith is really about. Christianity is not about big church buildings, Christian concerts with special effects or elaborate social programs. Instead, all that we are and everything we do is based on one single morning at a tomb. The body of Jesus was supposed to be inside it. The priests were counting on it because they had sent soldiers to guard it. Pilate was sure of it because it was shut with a Roman seal. Even the closest friends of Jesus believed He would be there because they went with spices to prepare the body. And the grave was shut. The tomb was silent. The death from crucifixion was final…. Until it wasn't!

"You seek Jesus who was crucified" the angel said. "He is not here for He has risen as He said!" And in that moment all History turned on the hinge of one simple miracle - an empty tomb and our risen Lord!

Day 22   Even Now

"Lord," Martha said to Jesus, "if you had been here, my brother would not have died. But I know that **even now** God will give you whatever you ask."
John 11:21-22 ESV

We often hear of Martha's faults and her worrying about pots and pans, but the Bible plainly tells us that Jesus loved Martha. Maybe one of the things Jesus loved so much about her was her outspoken way of speaking her mind. Whether she was complaining about her sister, inviting Jesus into her home, or sending for him in her time of need, Martha was always direct. She seemed to always have the unique ability to grow because she held nothing back. In our own Christian walk, we may feel it is easier to pray in a special religious way than to really tell God what we are thinking. We are trying to avoid conflict, but we are missing out on the opportunity to grow in our faith. We are hiding behind what we feel is acceptable yet denying Jesus the chance to enter into our struggles. But if like Martha we tell Him all our heart, **even now** He can still do more than we could ever imagine!

Day 23
The Fragrance of the Perfume

Then Mary took a pound of very costly oil of spikenard, anointed the feet of Jesus, and wiped His feet with her hair. And the house was filled with the fragrance of the oil. **John 12:3 NKJV**

While Hollywood has given us the impression that Mary was a beautiful young woman that may not have been the case. In that time, even poor beautiful women would have married and Mary was not poor. While we do not know Mary's age it is possible that she and Martha were both widows, living with their brother Lazarus. That would give us an entirely different view than the film version. In this scene we meet a Mary who kept all her savings in that perfume jar. It acted as something of a retirement account. As she grew older with no marital prospects or even the right to own property, that perfume was all she had besides the kindness of her brother. As she broke the jar open and its fragrance filled the room, people began one by one to realize how exorbitant and even a little crazy, what Mary was doing really was! Her family and friends grew silent. Then one by one the disciples, beginning with Judas, began to complain. "Why wasn't this sold ...and given to the poor?" But Jesus knew Mary's heart and while she remained silent at His feet, He defended her. Today we have little to describe how Peter or John, Andrew or Phillip worshiped, but that perfume from Mary's jar still fills our rooms with its fragrance after two thousand years!

Day 24   God Loves You!

For God so loved the world, that he gave his only Son, that whoever believes in him should not perish but have eternal life. **John 3:16 ESV**

Marie* wants to see you in the cafeteria after the message" they told me last week. As I went in to sit with her she began to cry and took hold of my hands saying, "God hates me!" Marie suffers from Parkinson's and that afternoon she was so depressed that she hadn't come in for our song and prayer time at the nursing home. She feels isolated from the world outside of the home. No old friends come to visit. No family stops by on her birthday or Christmas. But you and I still have the same good news to share that God gave to us and that I shared with her that afternoon. "No Marie! God loves you! For God so loved the world…" I continued desperately struggling to communicate the love of Jesus in a way that would touch her at that very moment. As we approach Easter, will we remember to go and take all the Marie's hands, look into their eyes and tell them that God really does care? He has not forgotten them. He has not left them alone. We may not be the greatest or most talented people but we each have the gift of God's love to share. Will we go? Will we keep sharing? All the Marie's and Bettys and Florence's and Bobs and Joes are out there waiting to hear. What will our answer be?

Day 25   Christ Our Life

Jesus said to her, "I am the resurrection and the life. Whoever believes in me, though he die, yet shall he live. **John 11:25 ESV**

After the death of her brother, Martha was overcome with grief. Compounding the weight of the sorrow was her conviction that if only Jesus had come; Lazarus would not have died. Like Martha many of us are passing through dark hours that feel as if they stretch out to our horizon. Our hope looks ahead towards heaven trusting that there we will begin to experience eternal life. But right here and right now, during our deepest sorrow, and most humiliating defeat Jesus says that He is our life - if we will only believe.

As we near the end of this 40-day journey called Lent, if we, like Martha leave our comfort zone behind to meet with Jesus He will talk with us. He has not forgotten us. He is ready right here and right now to bring us hope in any situation. Today His promise is that if we only believe, He will not only give us life some day in heaven; but He will become our resurrection and life right now.

Prayer: Father I have tried so hard in my darkest moments to just hang on and wish for the storms to pass. But you have not left me alone and I trust that you who once calmed the wind and waves can be my resurrection and my life today!

Day 26   The Last Healing

And when he heard that it was Jesus of Nazareth, he began to cry out and say, "Jesus, Son of David, have mercy on me!" **Mark 10:47 NKJV**

As Jesus begins His final journey towards Jerusalem, a blind man named Batimaeus hears the news and in desperation cries to Him for help. Breaking the decorum of his day he starts to shout as loudly as he can, trying to get Jesus' attention, no matter what anyone else thinks.

During His ministry Jesus had healed all kinds of people including the mother of the Apostle Peter's wife, the servant of a government official and a woman who touched his robe in a crowd. As He neared the end of His time on earth, He raised His friend Lazarus from the dead.

But in His last miraculous act recorded in the Bible, Jesus paused to heal a bind beggar named Bartimaeus. This blind man had no special credentials or connections except Jesus was passing by. The amazing hope He found is also for everyone who has no pedigree, political connections, or friends in high places. The mercy of Jesus comes only with the requirement that, like Bartimaeus, we ask with all our heart.

Jesus is as willing to stop for a jailer as for a prisoner. He hears the prayer of the surgeon as well as the patient. He bends his ear as closely to hear orphans as he does to the father of a nation. Our hope in Jesus Christ is based on one thing alone. He died for our sins and rose again. He is walking down our street and He is still inviting beggars to come to His side in His heavenly home!

Day 27   What is Your Treasure?

And he said to them, "Therefore every scribe who has been trained for the kingdom of heaven is like a master of a house, who brings out of his treasure what is new and what is old." **Matthew 13:52 ESV**

I started storytelling, with a class of boys at church called Royal Rangers, which was a program similar to Boy Scouts, that our denomination offered. My career began the day I signed our oldest son up for the five year old class. Since I was interested to see what his class was like, I stayed to see what was going on. The man leading the group was so delighted to have another adult around to help, that he disappeared on the third week and; ta-da, I became their new leader! Needless to say, my transition from, "Hey I want to help ', to "Great you're in charge!" was rough. But during the mayhem, God began to teach me how to get their attention with stories. In today's scripture, Jesus gives us the inside scoop on how to teach others about His kingdom, and He calls it giving away our treasure. So, what makes something our treasure? I have a piece of paper proving that I've been to college, but my most treasured lessons are from God rescuing me in the storms of life. He specializes in teaching in the classroom of our problems and there He gives us treasures of grace to share. Notice also, that Jesus says, we need both new and old treasures, so don't get comfortable because new storms are always on the horizon! So, whether you are trying to keep the attention of children or are having an on-line class with seniors who are struggling with their computers, God wants to use you to spread His treasure around. So, what is your story? Why not share your treasure today?

Day 28   Change the World!

As he passed by, he saw a man blind from birth. And his disciples asked him, "Rabbi, who sinned, this man or his parents, that he was born blind?" Jesus answered, "It was not that this man sinned, or his parents, but that the works of God might be displayed in him. **John 9:1-3 ESV**

It is popular to say that "Let's change the world!" and considering all the changes brought on by the virus, the political climate and upheaval in our society, we have certainly seen a lot of change. "But not all change is good, so let's ask, "How can we change the world for the better? Amazingly the one person, who has changed the world the most, never held political office, owned a home, or traveled the world. Instead, He talked about God, healed the sick and accepted the outcasts of his day. But when large crowds began following Jesus, He sent them away and went to a mountain to pray. In the Bible, we find that; Jesus was interested in changing the world, but His tactics were different than ours. Instead of finding the best arenas to fill, He went to people in need. The woman at the well and another about to be stoned each left His presence, changed. A young man about to be buried was raised from the dead (Now that's a change!) and a leper on the outskirts of a village was healed. In today's verse we meet an unnamed blind beggar. Maybe the Bible does not tell us his identity because we are all like him. We do not need to be important, rich, or talented and it doesn't matter what other people think about us.

God wants us to know that He hasn't forgotten about us and that our problems are not too hard for Him to solve. If we just trust Him, He will change us forever. Then through our lives, no matter what anyone else thinks, God will be glorified. Now tell me, what change is any better than that?!

Day 29   Just Before the Dawn

And after he had taken leave of them, he went up on the mountain to pray. And when evening came, the boat was out on the sea, and he was alone on the land. And he saw that they were making headway painfully, for the wind was against them. And about the fourth watch of the night, he came to them, walking on the sea. He meant to pass by them. **Mark 6:46-48**

Have you ever wondered why Jesus lets us get ourselves in a fix to begin with? Why do we find ourselves over and over in the middle of a sea of circumstances which we did not choose and wish we had never encountered? I know from the Bible that it is for my own good, but when I am rowing hard in the middle of a pitch-black night, I am not liking a lot what He says is good for me!

But in the middle of my feelings of confusion and helplessness, I have His promise that I am not forgotten. Jesus has been watching and praying for me and best of all, Jesus is coming to meet me just before the dawn!

Day 30   This is Going to Hurt!

For the Lord disciplines the one he loves, and chastises every son whom he receives. **Hebrews 12:7 ESV**

Maybe the phrase, "This is going to hurt me more than it's going to hurt you!" is imprinted indelibly in my memory, because it always preceded several well aimed smacks on my behind. It was not that I questioned the truth my stepfather's intentions, it was simply the fact that I never listened to any of the words that came after, and "This is going to hurt!" So, when I first came to this passage in Hebrews my mind slipped back in time to those moments of discipline, and I inwardly cringed as I waited for God's punishment to fall. Although we truly need to be disciplined by our heavenly Father, the reality is that it hurt God far more than it hurts us. God is correcting us for things we have done wrong, but Jesus went as an innocent lamb to the cross to pay for our adoption into His family. Like Thomas we worry that we have been left out of blessings that we think we deserve. But the good news is that Jesus came even for a doubtful Thomas. He showed him the marks of the nails in his hands and the scar from the spear in His side. It's as if He looked lovingly into Thomas' fearful eyes and said, "Stop your doubting and just believe. This really did hurt me more than it hurt you, but it was worth it because I want you to be my son!"

Day 31   Where is Our Hope?

Who has seen the wind? Neither you nor I
But when the trees bow down their heads
The wind is passing by
**Who Has Seen the Wind?
by Christina Rossetti**

I am not much for remembering long passages of verse, but tiny snippets like these come to mind when I am alone. This week, when I had been making a fuss about things I could not understand, I remembered that line, "But when the trees bow down their heads". Like the perfect Father that He is, God comforted me with this reminder that faith is the way He chooses for us to walk with Him. Sure, Moses saw the burning bush and Peter got to see Jesus transformed on the mountain. But for many of us, our faith is built on somewhat less spectacular experiences. In fact, Peter himself points out that our hope and joy is based on a Jesus whom we have never seen.

And though you have never seen him, yet I know that you love him. At present you trust him without being able to see him, and even now he brings you a joy that words cannot express, and which has in it a hint of the glories of Heaven;
1 Peter 1:8 Phillips Version

Some of you are struggling with loneliness, sickness, or heartache, wishing that Jesus would just show up and fix things. It would be great to see God swing into action like Spiderman, to save us from problems, but He has a better way! His solution does not depend on things we can see, but on the unseen love of Jesus Christ. We do not believe because we have seen, but because we have experienced God's gift of joy through a faith that gives us, "A hint of heaven" and God whispers, "That hint is more than enough!"

Day 32   Mustard Seed Faith

And the Lord said, "If you had faith like a grain of mustard seed, you could say to this mulberry tree, 'Be uprooted and planted in the sea,' and it would obey you. **Luke 17:6 ESV**

If you are a little like me, you may find yourself sometimes praying "Lord please, give me more faith!" When we feel like we are drowning in a sea of fear we try grasping at straws floating on the water's surface. But our good news for today is that Jesus does not require us to have a large quantity of faith.

In fact, during His time on earth, Jesus seemed to take special delight in people who struggled to believe. After watching the Lord multiply bread for five thousand men, the disciples were worried when they ran out of bread in their boat. He sat and talked to a woman by a well who probably never darkened the doors of her synagogue. He healed a man's son after the father confessed his unbelief and made a special appearance for Thomas when he refused to believe the others about the resurrection.

So, on nights when it feels like you are going under for the third time, remember that our Lord loves to walk out on the water in the middle of storms. He came for the widow, the orphan, and the poor. Jesus is moved when we pray with even a tiny seed of faith. When we move the heart of God in prayer, we will discover that He is ready to move anything in our path.

Day 33   Getting Back in the Boat

And when they got into the boat, the wind ceased. **Matthew 14:32 NKJV**

This short verse from Matthew's gospel held a promise for me that I had overlooked till I desperately needed it. My mother was just sixty-two when she died of breast cancer and her passing left me feeling like I had been run over by a truck. The years struggling to rebuild our relationship, the prayers and the conversations were suddenly over. I felt as if I were locked in a room with barely enough air to breathe. I sleepwalked through months of guilt and regret for what had never been. I had often thought about God challenging me as He had challenged Peter to get out of the boat. At other times I had been comforted knowing that just as Jesus had reached out his hand to save Peter, He would take my hand in the middle of a crisis. But it was just as important for me to learn that Jesus wanted to help me back into the boat and restore calm when this storm had passed. I do not know how it happened but gradually light began shining in the dark places of my heart. I woke up to find that though I might never understand the why behind the pain, knowing only God knew had become enough

Do we struggle to see God as more than just challenging or rescuing us? What a wonderful surprise awaits when we realize that He is also delighted to help us back in the boat and calm our winds to a hush.

Day 34   Faces in the Crowd

Therefore, since we are surrounded by such a huge crowd of witnesses to the life of faith, let us strip off every weight that slows us down, especially the sin that so easily trips us up. And let us run with endurance the race God has set before us. **Hebrews 12:1 NLT**

Back in 2016 the Olympic flame was carried by over 10,000 runners. The torch run which began in the capital city of Brasilia went the distance of 20,000 kilometers throughout the nation to Rio de Janeiro. Some of the way they passed through city neighborhoods lined with crowds, and others, over empty farmland and forest. All along the way the torch bearers ran till Vanderlei de Lima lit the flame before a crowd of over 60,000 in Maracanã Stadium.

In that same way as we run the race of our Christian life there are some lonely times. It feels as if the finish line in Heaven's capital city is impossibly far away. God's word encourages us to recall that God has a stadium there also filled with the faces of those who have carried their torches before us. We have parents, and pastors, brothers, sisters, wives, and children waiting and cheering us on. They were not all saintly and perfect people, but they carried the torch to the end. They climbed the steps to the throne of God and left everything behind to finish their race. In the light of their flame of faith I can see their faces and am reminded to trust that God will help me run my own leg of the journey one more day!

Day 35   My Easter Miracle

The saying is trustworthy and deserving of full acceptance, that Christ Jesus came into the world to save sinners, of whom I am the foremost. **1 Timothy 1:15 ESV**

In 1971 I was just another 19-year-old hippie trying to figure life out. One night I found myself along a lonely stretch of desert highway between L.A. and Phoenix. All that day I had hitch-hiked with my last ride dropping me off at a rest area. As night began to fall, I reasoned that the top of one of the picnic tables was the safest refuge from snakes and scorpions. So, I rolled out my sleeping bag and struggled into it trying not to fall off the edge of the table. There I lay looking up into a vast sky filled with stars wondering where I belonged and fell asleep. How I ended up 3,000 miles from home was a tangle of events beginning with parents who seemed more confused about life than I was. I had moved out on my own at age seventeen and began a journey that brought me that morning to a highway rest stop. There I met a car load of young people who invited me to church. It would have taken a miracle to break through my fears and excuses; but, with the added bonus of a promised free meal after church, I eagerly agreed to go. Their church was different than anything I expected. It was filled with young people who were singing with smiles that showed me they knew something about Easter that I didn't. More importantly, for the first time I considered that God just might be real and actually care about me. I had been running away all my life and I couldn't run any more. It took an amazing chain of miracles to bring me to God. But it was Easter and on Easter miracles happen!

Day 36   Crossing the Bridge

I will instruct you and teach you in the way you should go; I will counsel you with my eye upon you **Psalm 32:8 ESV**

When I was young, our parents often took my sister and me to the museums in New York. We were hoping to see dinosaurs, but they felt it was more important for us to see the Museum of Fine Art, the Guggenheim and other places filled with paintings. One day after visiting the Pratt Institute of Art in Brooklyn they decided to cross over to Manhattan. I heard my mom say, "Look, there's the Empire State building. Just head that way and we'll get there!" So, my stepdad started across Brooklyn towards that landmark. While he drove, I heard him say, "Why should I stop to ask directions. They always tell me to turn around and go the other way!" So, they kept driving, always keeping the spire of the building in view. Sadly, when we came to the river, my parents realized discovered they had forgotten something: they needed to cross a bridge! We are all like that when we forget we need to cross God's bridge. Today's verse teaches us that finding God's direction, means first we must stopping to ask. We may putting this off, like my step-dad, because we are afraid, He will say to turn around. But God promises that if we do, He will guide us every step of the way. Then God says He will guide us with His loving eye. He is not just wanting to control us like a remote-control car but is watching to protect us from harm. Lastly, we can know that He is lovingly watching over us because when we open the door He gets in and rides with us all the way across the river!

Day 37   The Rooster Crowed

And Peter remembered the saying of Jesus, "Before the rooster crows, you will deny me three times." And he went out and wept bitterly.
Matthew 26:75 ESV

In the pre-dawn hours after the arrest of Jesus, Peter was determined to see if he could find a way to free him. He followed the soldiers as they led Jesus into the courtyard of the high priest, but as he entered a young servant girl who was watching asked curiously, "Weren't you one of those who was with Jesus?" Peter turned, frustrated in being distracted in his purpose and answered, "No, not me. You must be mistaken." Then He moved on trying to think of what he could do, when another person stopped him saying., "I am sure I saw you with him!" But Peter shook his head again, "No way! I don't know that man." Finally, as he worked his way closer to Jesus, Peter tried questioning people to find out what was going on, but just then someone tapped him on the shoulder saying, "Hey buddy, I can tell by your accent, that you are from Galilee. You are one His disciples!" "Me. Are you kidding?" Peter answered angrily and began to curse and swear. Then a rooster crowed and Peter remembered what Jesus had said and at that exact moment, Jesus turned to look at him. Then Peter realized how miserably he had failed and ran out weeping. But just as Jesus forgave and restored Peter, He is willing to do the same for us. We have hope because just as Jesus knew that Peter would fail, He also knew how He would give His life so that both we and Peter could be restored!

Day 38   Master There's More

And while he was at Bethany in the house of Simon the leper, as he was reclining at table, a woman came with an alabaster flask of ointment of pure nard, very costly, and she broke the flask and poured it over his head. **Mark 14:3 ESV**

Then Mary took a pound of very costly oil of spikenard, anointed the feet of Jesus, and wiped His feet with her hair. And the house was filled with the fragrance of the oil. **John 12:3 NKJV**

I had long been puzzled by the differences in the stories of the anointing of Jesus at Bethany. As I began to re-imagine the scene at the banquet. I saw Lazarus seated next to Jesus, with Martha serving the tables as the people slowly filled the room. Then Mary appeared in the doorway, holding her alabaster jar of perfumed oil. Silently she slipped through to where

Jesus reclined, and broke the seal on her jar pouring some on the head of Jesus. The power of the fragrance immediately filled the room. A momentary silence ensued as the guests stopped and turned to see what had happened. But then just as quickly, the air was filled with complaints about such a waste of resources being made. Mary kneels unashamed looking up to Jesus' face and seeing His acceptance of her gift, she pours the rest of the perfumed oil on His feet and wipes them clean with her hair. Instead of worrying about what others thought, Mary focused on only one thing. She still had more for Jesus! As we are traveling together towards the Passion of Christ this month, we should also ask; "Am I too worried about what everyone else will say?, or can I say with Mary, "Master there's still more!"

Day 39   Not Lost in the Crowd

When he went ashore he saw a great crowd, and he had compassion on them, because they were like sheep without a shepherd. And he began to teach them many things. **Mark 6:34 ESV**

After these last two years, many of us are mentally and physically worn out. During the pandemic, many have lost friends and family to the virus and are experiencing isolation and feel forgotten and lost in the crowd. Jesus felt all of that and more after receiving the news that his cousin, John the Baptist had been beheaded. With so many people surrounding him hoping for their own miracles, neither Jesus, nor His disciples even have a chance to eat. So when Jesus suggested that they go somewhere to get away and rest, the disciples probably broke out into a happy dance shouting, "Amen!" But as they stepped out of the boat at their getaway location,

Jesus looked out and saw that the crowd had followed them. You might think that He would see those people as a burden, but instead, today's verse says, "He had compassion on them because they were like sheep without a shepherd." He did not just see a crowd, He saw people. Considering that today there are 7.6 billion in the crowd, aren't you glad that He knows you by name and wants to be your shepherd? A good shepherd always makes sure His sheep get fed, and that is exactly what Jesus did. Remember that the disciples had not eaten since the day before? They would have been delighted to see the crowds leave. But instead, Jesus began to teach them to shepherd others.

He could have just said, "Give me a loaf of bread!" and presto! – done everything by himself. Instead, He asked them to help by handing out the bread, one piece at a time so that no one would be lost in the crowd that day.

Day 40
Palm Sunday Your King is Coming

This took place to fulfill what was spoken by the prophet, saying, and "Say to the daughter of Zion, 'Behold, your king is coming to you, humble, and mounted on a donkey, on a colt, the foal of a beast of burden.
Matthew 21:4-5 ESV

When we think of Palm Sunday, we see it as the triumphant end of a week in which Jesus had raised Lazarus from the dead and healed a blind man on the way to Jerusalem. But for the first century Jew it was also the beginning of a festival week. Try to imagine the week before Christmas. People are doing extra baking, decorating the house, and inviting friends and family over for the big day. And right through the middle of the excited crowds, Jesus rode into the Eastern Gate of Jerusalem. Although the religious elite were angry when children shouted Hosanna, the common people sensed something their leaders missed. Jesus humbly coming to them riding a donkey was not just coming to town for the Passover. He was coming to fulfill the prophecy of how God would send their king to them riding on a donkey through that gate. He was more amazing than a miracle worker, more powerful than a prophet, and greater than any religious leader. Jesus was their Messiah and king!

Day 41   Monday - House Cleaning

And he was teaching them and saying to them, "Is it not written, 'My house shall be called a house of prayer for all the nations'? But you have made it a den of robbers." **Mark 11:17 ESV**

Some of us get the idea that Jesus of Nazareth went through His ministry smiling, blessing children, and sitting with lambs. But on Monday of Holy Week; this same Jesus who had forgiven the woman caught in adultery and sat down to eat with sinners, became angry when He went to the temple. He found at the entrance a group of people setting up shop in hopes of making a quick buck. Then gentle Jesus made a whip and started driving them out shouting, "Is it not written My House shall be called a house of prayer for all nations?" Now the case could be made that Jesus was upset about the physical location where these vendors were set up. But when Jesus used the word "House" it meant household. In other words, the place where God's family meets should be exclusively for coming together to pray. It is easy for us to criticize them, but do we sometimes maneuver our way into strategic positions in order to take advantage of others? Can we say with all honesty that prayer is the main thing that happens when we go to church? Jesus went on to say that His family was also supposed to include all nations. Are all nations showing up at our place of worship or are we separated by factions, unwilling to pray together? Yes Jesus is still humble and gentle, but He is also Holy and angry at anyone who hurts His family and everyone who works to keep us apart.

Day 42 – Holy Tuesday
Jesus Sees a Woman's Heart

Jesus looked up and saw the rich putting their gifts into the offering box, and he saw a poor widow put in two small copper coins. And he said, "Truly, I tell you, this poor widow has put in more than all of them. **Luke 21:1-3 ESV**

On this, His final day of public ministry, Jesus took the time to praise the offering of a widow. Among the crowds at the temple that day, she was probably considered the least important by most people. Few would have even noticed as she quietly slipped her two coins into the charity box. But everyone saw the rich men as they carried in their gifts with great fanfare. At the sound of their silver and gold coins clanking into the box people were oohing and aahing about how much they gave. But Jesus was not impressed with their money. He did not care about their spectacular performance or false religiosity. Yet He took time to see this widow just before He sat down for His last meal. He pointed her out for all of us to see, because she had come and humbly given with all of her heart. Then He broke the bread and gave the cup and gave His own life for you and for me.

Day 43   Holy Wednesday
One Scrub at a Time

Then he poured water into a basin and began to wash the disciples' feet and to wipe them with the towel that was wrapped around him. **John 13:5 ESV**

One of the most humbling experiences of our mission trip in India happened in a small village, where we distributed free dental hygiene kits for children. We met at a church that consisted of nothing more than a tin roof with rough boards for siding and carpets laid over the dirt floor. At the end of the service a girl of about 13 years old came to the front and with tears of gratitude thanked us for our visit. Then with the help of a friend she began to wash our feet. I have never felt so unworthy by their beautiful expression of the love of Jesus. But as moving as that moment was, I have learned that it is easier to travel thousands of miles, to serve someone than it is to remember those closest to us. In today's verse you will notice that Jesus did not go out looking for people to serve, He simply took off His robe of a Rabbi and put on the towel of a servant and began washing the dirty feet nearest to Him. So if you are wondering how you can "Change the world", don't wait to go overseas on a missions trip. We have an invitation from God to wash dirty feet that are closest to us today. If that seems hard, then imagine how Jesus felt while He was washing the feet of Judas - His betrayer, Peter His Denier and Thomas His doubter. And yet the Son of God put aside all He had to show them His love as one scrub at a time He washed their dirty their feet!

Prayer: Here are my hands Lord – may You use them to wash dirty feet today!

Day 44   Maundy Thursday

And he said to them, "I have earnestly desired to eat this Passover with you before I suffer. **Luke 22:15 ESV**

Maundy Thursday is the most overlooked day of Easter Week. But for Jesus this was the crucial time to prepare His disciples for His departure. At the Last Supper Jesus gave the New Covenant to both His friends and through them to us who are believers today. Every time we take communion in our various churches, we continue to remember His death and atonement as people have done for 2,000 years. At the Last Supper Jesus gave not only a New Covenant but He also set the example for a new lifestyle.

While those we consider saints today were arguing over who was the most important, Jesus went and filled a basin with water and began to wash their feet.

When their meal was over, Jesus led His eleven faithful disciples to the Garden of Gethsemane to pray. There He fully and finally accepted His coming death on the cross. There He woke them again and again and urged them to pray also until Judas came with the soldiers. And then the hour had come for His sacrifice. When everyone ran away, in that garden, Jesus stayed behind as the Lamb of God to take away our sins.

Day 45   Good Friday

And walk in love, as Christ loved us and gave himself up for us,
a fragrant offering and sacrifice to God.
Ephesians 5:2 ESV

When I think of Good Friday and the cross I often remember the prayer that Jesus prayed in Gethsemane just the night before. In HIs simple but passionate plea, Jesus humbled His awesome power that had commanded wind and waves and raised the dead and accepted in loving trust the terrible death of the cross. We need to remind ourselves that He could have hidden himself when they came to arrest Him or struck down a thousand soldiers by a single word. Instead, He prayed until He sweat blood and yielded Himself to His Father's will. He took the shame and suffering of the cross because of His great love for us. Now He could have prayed in sullen acceptance; "I know I have to die Father. So, let's just get this over with." But instead, Jesus yielded His heart and chose the Father's will. That humbles me when I recall, how often I have prayed and given grudgingly but without surrender. I may not choose disobedience, but I still miss the mark of true love. But because of Jesus' loving obedience, Peter came to repentance, Nicodemus had the opportunity to be courageous and a thief found a home in paradise. A rich man had the chance to learn how to give and Mary Magdalene got to be the first to see Him risen and alive. They all received because Jesus gave himself and they became a part of the fragrance of the sacrifice of Jesus. So, what about this morning?

Will we surrender whatever is in our hands today to God? Will we willingly let go of what is ours to gain something for others? Will we surrender and follow our Lord and offer a sacrifice with a sweet fragrance to God today?

Day 46 Holy Saturday
A Borrowed Tomb

This man went unto Pilate and begged the body of Jesus. And he took it down, and wrapped it in linen, and laid it in a sepulchre that was hewn in stone, wherein never man before was laid.
Luke 23:52-53 KJV

When Jesus was born, Mary wrapped Him in swaddling cloths and laid him in a manger because there was no room at the inn. At death Joseph of Arimathea took him down from the cross, wrapped Him in linens and put Jesus in his tomb because there was nowhere else. While Jesus was traveling one day a man rushed up to ask if he could follow, and Jesus answered by making it clear that to be a disciple meant accepting the fact that often Jesus had nowhere to lay his head. From birth till death, there was no place that Jesus belonged. But that is a wonderful story not a sad one, because we find out that Jesus had a far better home than earth and far more beautiful clothing than linens or swaddling cloths.

On Holy Saturday, Jesus was laid in a borrowed tomb, but He did not make it His home. He said He was going to His Father's house to live and prepare a place for anyone who would follow. Have you decided to follow Jesus? Then remember; this earth is not our home either. We have one that has all the taxes paid, that never needs repair, and that God has reserved in heaven for anyone who will trust Jesus and follow Him to the end!

Day 47 Easter Sunday
Meeting Jesus

His head and his hairs were white like wool, as white as snow; and his eyes were as a flame of fire
Revelation 1:14 KJV

On the first Easter Sunday, Mary Magdalene met Jesus outside of the tomb. Jesus was right there, but until He revealed himself to her, she thought He was just the gardener. What is Jesus really like? What would it be like to meet with Jesus? John the Apostle says of his own unexpected meeting with Jesus on the Island of Patmos. "And when I saw him, I fell at his feet as dead…" Revelation 1:17 KJVa

It was too overwhelming seeing Jesus even for a moment! But Jesus came and put out his hand to touch John and said:

"Fear not; I am the first and the last."
Revelation 1:17 KJV

Jesus knows every detail of our lives, and He wants us to know Him. Easter Sunday means finding Jesus is not only alive, but alive and wanting us to know Him. Are you waiting outside a tomb of dying hopes and wondering where Jesus is today? The message of Easter is that He will come just when we least expect it. He knows all about us and He wants to come and change our lives forever! What a wonderful Risen Lord and Savior we have waiting for us again this Easter!

God Gently Stooped Down

Who is like the Lord our God, the One who sits enthroned on high, who stoops down to look on the heavens and the earth? **Psalm 113:5-6, NIV**

When at Bethlehem's stable God gently stooped down
He entered our world in the dark of that town
And on a hill and a cross He stooped lower still
Took the nails and the thorns so that we could be healed

Then sadly His friends took Him down from the tree
And put Him in the tomb where no one could see
But Christ rose from the dead just before the third dawn
When God rolled back the stone
As He gently stooped down!

About the Author

Peter Caligiuri has been writing since he was a teen-ager. Both short poems and devotionals have appeared in various periodicals such Secret Place, Breakthrough Intercessor and The Upper Room. Peter holds a Bachelor of Science in Secondary Education/English from Western Connecticut State College as well as having attended Elim Bible College. He is now retired and lives with his wife Nancy in New Port Richey Florida where they are members of Generations Christian Church. Together they have two awesome sons, six lively grandsons and one very special granddaughter!

Devotional Resources

Thank you for spending time as together we have walked through this Easter season. Here is a collections of devotional writing for Christmas as well as an illustrated book of children's book of poetry. These are available in both eBook and paperback from Kindle Direct Publishing (KDP) @ Amazon.com.

All Creatures Mostly Small – A child's look at the creation and its creator with poems of hummingbirds and eagles and even our ears and nose all showing the glory of God. My young friend Emilia has given us, by her amazing artwork, a way to see some big things God wants to show us by the smallest members of His creation.

Finding Jesus This Christmas - We are called to seek Him not only at Christmas, but also on our sunniest of mornings and the darkest of our nights. He is the friend of sinners and He is Immanuel – God with us! That is why we can celebrate and trust our hearts to Him. Why not join with me as we set our hearts over these next thirty days in seeking to find Jesus This Christmas?

Made in the USA
Monee, IL
20 February 2022

91540210R00059